Christmas and the Good Turn Diary

Christmas and the Good Turn Diary

James E. Faust

DESERET
BOOK

SALT LAKE CITY, UTAH

Design: Meridith Ethington
Cover illustration: Jay Bryant Ward

© 2006 Intellectual Reserve, Inc.

DESERET BOOK is a registered trademark of Deseret Book Company.

Visit us at deseretbook.com

ISBN-10 1-59038-700-7
ISBN-13 978-1-59038-700-9

Printed in the United States of America
Artistic Printing, Salt Lake City, Utah

10   9   8   7   6   5   4   3   2   1

AT THIS CHRISTMAS SEASON, I extend warmest greetings to every-one. I pray that sacred memories of happy holiday times in our lives will be repeated for each of us this season. As the years pass, special memories are often more of happenings than of things.

I say this because many of my happy childhood memories occurred during the

difficult economic times of the great Depression. The extraordinary unselfishness brought out in people unforgettable concern for others. Members of families had to pool income and resources to survive. I recall one of my uncles who had a job working for the railroad used to send his uncashed paycheck to Grandfather to meet the needs of the family. The difficulties of life made us rise above our selfish desires.

When I came home from my mission my Uncle Jim told me about an exceptional young lady who worked with him. This woman gave her mother money out of her paycheck to pay for her mother's mortgage on the home. If I had not married that

special young lady I think my Uncle Jim would have wanted to!

I wish to tell a true story that happened during the 1930s to a family in Canada. Frigid weather gripped their town, and the Cards' ten-room, two-story house stood cold, all closed off except for the bathroom, kitchen, and dining room, which were meagerly heated by the coal-burning stove in the kitchen. I now turn to Brother Lincoln Card's own words:

"A Christmas tree crowded the corner of the dining room. My older brothers had tied a rope from the hinge of the door leading to the front entry hall, then diagonally across the room to the hinge of the

door leading to the kitchen. From this rope hung ten limp, well-worn stockings, many of them filled from heel to toe with loving stitches. . . .

"I was eight years old and had saved every penny since the past February in order to buy presents for my family.

"My oldest brother, Brigham, had been working on a government highway project high in the Rocky Mountains of southern Alberta. He had sent all of his earnings home to my father to help the family survive the stranglehold of financial depression.

"Today, however, was Christmas morning, and the laughing excitement of eight

children electrified the air as they lined up at the kitchen door awaiting Father's signal to enter the magical Christmas room. Enchantment had swallowed up the harried struggles for survival of the past year.

"'Open the door!'

"This signal brought cheers of delight as eight eager children flew to their stockings.

"For a fleeting moment, I had a feeling of disappointment as the stockings appeared to look as limp and lifeless as they had been on Christmas Eve. However, on closer observation my disappointment turned to thrilling delight as I recognized some small bulges stretching the sides of

the otherwise gaunt stockings. A comb, a pair of socks, a toothbrush, a pair of shoelaces, some handkerchiefs, a few nuts, and most of all the wonderful hard-tack candy, with colored stripes and designs.

"A feeling of love, excitement, and joy filled the room.

"From the corner of my eye, I noticed Father open a plain, wrapped, small gift. It was a [small Scout diary, about the size that could be carried in a] shirt pocket. As he fingered through the pages, his cheerful smile melted into thoughtful reflection. Tears began to dazzle his eyes, overflowing in little bursts of silver down the crease of

his weary, worn cheeks. Quickly, he left the room. . . .

"Soon Father reappeared. His countenance was subdued and calm. There was a glow about him as if he had seen some heavenly vision. He walked slowly to his stocking, bowed his head for a moment, and then slowly raised it. In a composed and gentle voice, he called out: 'I would like to have everyone's attention.'

"This unusual request on a Christmas morning brought quick silence from eight children and Mother. All eyes were fixed on Father in the wonderment of expectation. Slowly he raised his hand, which held the little well-worn book, and spoke. The

sound of his voice rang with a mellow yet driving sincerity that seemed to infuse my very being. 'I have just been given the greatest Christmas gift that I have ever received.'

"There was a short pause as he blinked away the mists that blurred his vision. Then he continued: 'I want to tell you all about it. This is a gift from your brother Brigham. It is a little [Boy Scout diary] with [the initials GT printed on] each day of this year. In the front of the book is a note which says, "Dear Father, I had no money to buy gifts this year. This is all I have to give you. [Each crossed out GT is] a record

of a good [turn] which I have done for someone each day of the year."'

"Father then stopped speaking. A hush fell over the whole family.

"The impact from the message of this gift left us all in thoughtful, reverent silence. Then someone began to clap their hands. Soon everyone was clapping with the joy of having experienced such an inspirational moment.

"Though many years have passed since that eventful Christmas morning, the impact of its message of service and love lingers on as a brilliant, guiding star."

The initials GT printed on the right-hand side of each page in the little scout

diary stood for "good turn." As the scout did his daily good turn he would cross through those initials to indicate to himself that he had done it. Even though Brigham had done a good deed each day, no details were given of them in this little scout diary of 1933, but it is noted that he had crossed through every GT throughout the year!

One or two entries from the diary itself are poignant, however, considering how hard he had to work for so little pay. For example, on December 20th Brigham wrote, "Picked sugar beets all day, sub zero weather all morning, mud in afternoon." Then on Christmas Day, he wrote: "Santa was good. The children all were happy.

Aaron got a wagon. Lester a suit. Ruth a pen and stockings, Rhea and Marie a doll and bed. Lincoln a truck and gas station. Eldon a scarf, underwear, a cap. BY a scarf, pen, gloves, writing paper, hanky. Mother a dressing gown, Father a key ring, tie, socks, etc. We had the Reids to Christmas dinner. Had a good time." Brother Brigham Card, now ninety years old, kindly loaned me this old scout diary he gave his father as a Christmas present so long ago. It still records the crossed out GT for each day of the year 1933, showing he did a good deed for someone else each day of the year.

We are each the agents of our Father in Heaven to do Christlike deeds for all His

Father's children, even as He offered to do in the grand premortal council when He said, "Here am I, send me."

"Father, thy will be done, and the glory be thine forever."

May the peace of heaven be ours this special time of year.